I. Introduction

Retail bank deposits are an important store of value in the United States—totaling over $6 trillion –and are the sole store of wealth for many U.S. households, particularly less wealthy ones. According to the 2010 Survey of Consumer Finances (SCF), about two-thirds of households in the bottom income quintile had bank deposits as assets, while only a single-digit percentage of such households had any holdings in other liquid financial assets.[2] Taken together, these facts suggest that changes in deposit rates may have economically significant effects on consumers.

Researchers have long studied the behavior of deposit rates. Hannan and Berger (1991), Neumark and Sharpe (1992), Diebold and Sharpe (1990), Craig and Dinger (2011), and Yankov (2012) have shown that rates may take months to change and respond asymmetrically to changes in banks' costs of funds (as proxied by the federal funds rate or other interest rates): deposit rates are upwards-sticky but downwards-flexible. In this paper, we complement this work by using a high-frequency (weekly) panel dataset observed over a ten-year period for over 2,500 branches of about 900 depository institutions (DIs) for ten different types of deposit rates.[3] Given this sample, which is both longer and broader than most of those previously used, we are able to more precisely estimate the duration between interest rate changes and to document the asymmetry of price adjustment over the course of two full FOMC easing and tightening cycles. The large number of DI branches allows us to study differences in rate-changing behavior across institutions; this sort of evidence complements the typical approach in the literature on price-setting, which looks at changes in the prices of many goods at a single firm or of single goods

---

[2] Holdings of non-bank financial assets, with the exception of the cash value of life insurance, only reach double digit rates for the third quintile of income and above. See Bricker et al. (2012) for further details.

[3] Depository institutions include banks as well as thrifts and credit unions.

averaged over many firms. We also document the sluggishness of deposit rate adjustment at the aggregate level.

We have six key findings. First, some deposit rates are more flexible than others. Rates on certificates of deposits (CDs) – are quite flexible, with the median institution changing such rates every 6 to 7 weeks on average. Rates on money market deposit accounts (MMDAs) and interest checking accounts show much more inertia, changing every 20 weeks and 37 weeks on average, respectively. By comparison, the target federal funds rate – an important determinant of DIs' cost of funds, and thus a good proxy for DI marginal cost – changed about every 12 weeks across the period. Second, the frequency of rate changes exhibits considerable dispersion for some types of deposits, with about a quarter of institutions changing interest checking rates twice a year or less frequently. Third, deposit rate changes are asymmetric: at the institution level, rates adjust about twice as frequently during periods of falling target federal funds rates as they do in rising ones. Fourth, rates are uniformly quite sticky during periods when the federal funds rate is flat, with median durations between price changes ranging from 7 weeks to 37 weeks. Fifth, the median size of rate changes is 11 to 23 basis points, comparable to the typical 25 basis point change in the target federal funds rate; the distribution of average decreases and increases is about the same, and is relatively dispersed, with many small changes of a few basis points. Sixth, there is a somewhat greater degree of upward stickiness in rates on interest checking and money market accounts for branches of large DIs than for branches of smaller ones.

We use the results that rates adjust only partially in the weeks and months following an increase in the target federal funds rate to calculate the costs to consumers of sluggish deposit rate adjustment. We find those costs to be on the order of about $100 billion per year during periods when the target federal funds rate rises. With deposit rates near zero as of late 2013, these calculations might be of particular interest as the date of liftoff for the federal funds target rate approaches.[4]

We also develop and calibrate a simple menu cost model that, for reasonable parameter values, can generate the sorts of asymmetric, sluggish adjustment seen in the data.

The rest of the paper proceeds as follows. We provide details on our dataset in section II. In section III, we document the sluggishness and asymmetry of deposit rate adjustment at the aggregate level over the past two decades, which includes two episodes of monetary policy tightening and easing, and we present some rough estimates of dollar value of the gap between sticky and equilibrium deposit rates. In section IV, we discuss deposit rate behavior at the microeconomic level. Section V relates our work to previous work on deposit rates. Section VI presents a simple static menu cost model that yields asymmetric, sluggish price adjustment. Section VII concludes.

II. Data

The core dataset of this paper is a proprietary weekly micro dataset of bank and thrift deposit rate data that is collected by Bankrate, Inc.[5] This dataset covers several thousand branches of nearly 900 DIs over a time span of about ten years, from the week of September 19, 1997 through the week of March 2, 2007. Data for each branch have the parent institution's NIC identification code as well as indicators of the banking market. The dataset has rates on interest-bearing checking accounts, money market deposit accounts (MMDAs), and nine

---

[4] As of September 2013, the FOMC's most recent Survey of Economic Projections indicated that the majority of meeting participants expected liftoff to occur in 2015, with projections ranging from 2014 to 2016. http://www.federalreserve.gov/monetarypolicy/files/fomcprojtabl20130918.pdf.

[5] http://www.bankrate.com. This dataset is available to users within the Federal Reserve System but, in accordance with the Federal Reserve Board's contract with Bankrate, Inc., cannot be shared with users outside the Federal Reserve. These data can be purchased directly from the company.

different maturities of certificates of deposit (CDs): 3, 6, 12, 24, 30, 36, 48, 60, and 84 months. The set of branches that provide data is not fully consistent from week to week due to mergers, exit and entry, and observations of zero, which we believe to be missing observations. The dataset begins with 443,189 observations, or an average of 897 cross-sectional observations for each of the 494 weeks in the sample. A relatively small number of observations suffered from certain irregularities, which we treated as follows.

First, some observations appeared to be partial or full duplicates of others, as if one observation sometimes contained a partially-completed survey and a separate observation contained the full set of information. We identified and dropped about 800 such duplicates, bringing the sample size to 442,407. Second, some observations also were incomplete but were followed by one or more additional observations with the same bank identification number and market rank and complementary data. Combining these observations eliminated about 22,000 observations and brought the sample size to 419,881 observations. Finally, we deleted the 55 observations that contained data for only one week, leaving us with 419,826 observations. The remaining dataset contained information on rates of 2,770 branches for 897 DIs.

A. Comparison with other data sources

One other source of interest rate data at the bank level has been used in previous work. Hannan and Berger (1991) and Neumark and Sharpe (1992) used the Federal Reserve's Monthly Survey of Selected Deposits and Other Accounts (also known as the FR 2042; hereafter the Monthly Survey). The survey collected the most commonly offered rate by account type; starting in 1989, the surveys allowed for the possibility that higher rates were offered for larger balances, a policy known as tiering. The Monthly Survey stopped collecting information on offered interest rates in 1994 and was discontinued in 1997.

An additional potential source of deposit rate data is the quarterly Consolidated Reports on Condition and Income, known more generally as the Call Reports. These quarterly financial statements, available since 1934, do not provide direct measures of deposit rates for commercial banks.[6] However, one can divide the interest expenses paid by the bank by the quantity of deposits in the account to obtain a weighted average of interest rates paid. A disadvantage is that, in the case of time deposits, the rate may not reflect current offered rates. Another disadvantage is that some categories of deposits are combined.[7]

An advantage of using the Bankrate data over the Monthly Survey is that the longer time series allows us to more accurately estimate longer durations of price stickiness. Moreover, the weekly frequency of the data allows us to see changes at a higher frequency than either the Monthly Survey or the Call Reports. A further advantage is that this data is collected for a wider variety of deposit types than other sources: we observe data on interest checking accounts, MMDAs, and CDs with nine different maturities. Finally, the Bankrate data is collected for a much larger group of DIs than the monthly survey, and at the branch level, allowing for better cross-sectional comparisons.

A significant disadvantage of the Bankrate data is that it appears to reflect only the lowest rate offered by deposit type. Rice and Ors (2006) document that the Bankrate data, on average, has significantly lower rates than the quarterly call report-based measures, suggesting that a substantial fraction of deposits are paid at higher rates.

---

[6] The comparable reports for savings and loans (thrifts) do provide direct measures of offered deposit rates.

[7] In part to avoid having deposit liabilities that are subject to reserve requirements, over the period analyzed, some banks "sweep" balances from reservable liabilities to non-reservable ones overnight, restoring them the following morning. This sweeping makes measurements of particular account types difficult. The Call Reports deal with this problem by aggregating reservable and non-reservable types of accounts.

The discrepancy in the average level of rates among datasets may not be completely problematic for our purposes. First, it is not clear that the stickiness properties of the rates on the bottom tier are different from those on upper tiers. As we show below, rates are sticky both at the aggregate level and the microeconomic level, suggesting that the Bankrate data is capturing the degree of price inflexibility appropriately. Second, although most deposits are likely paid at higher tiers, it is not clear that most depositors are receiving such rates, since the distribution of holdings across consumers is not uniform. To establish the importance of tiering, we surveyed 10 large banks and thrifts and 10 small banks and thrifts listed at the Bankrate website, which has more information on deposit rates by tier, to find average tiering levels. We found that the median levels at which tiering starts was $5,000 for MMDAs and interest checking accounts and $10,000 for CDs. Next, we used data from the 2004 Survey of Consumer Finances (SCF) to determine what fractions of households who hold those types of deposits have holdings below the tiering level. We find that about 76 percent of households with interest checking accounts have balances below the first tier cutoff of $5,000; for savings accounts and CDs, the analogous figures are 60 percent and 36 percent respectively. We conclude that the Bankrate interest rates are economically meaningful to a large number of households.[8]

III. Behavior of Aggregate Deposit Rate Data

A. Overview

We begin by showing that stickiness of deposit rate data is apparent even at the aggregate level. Figure 1 illustrates the slow asymmetric adjustment of aggregate deposit rates to market rates. The figure plots the time series of the overall return to M2, the heavy gray line, and

---

[8] Ratewatch.com, and additional source of banking data, including deposit and loan rates and fees, provides rate data at various tiers. The sample period is shorter than that for the Bankrate.com data.

returns to small time deposits and liquid deposits, the gray dashed lines, along with the federal funds target rate and the three-month Treasury bill rate, the blue and black lines, respectively.[9] Notably, over 2001, the federal funds target declined precipitously, while deposit rates initially declined more slowly than the target rate but then began to keep pace with the declines in the target rate. As the target rate rose beginning in late 2004, deposit rates rose much more slowly.

To better highlight the asymmetry of deposit rate adjustment, Figure 2 breaks up Figure 1 into periods during which the federal funds rate is falling or flat (upper panel), rising or flat (lower panel). The upper panel shows that deposit rates fall by closer to the same amount as the target federal funds rate, and the declines begin sooner after the initial decline in the federal funds rate. The lower panel shows that the M2 own rate, liquid deposit rate, and small-time deposit rate increases by much less than the corresponding increases in the federal funds rate; moreover, the M2 own rate continues to be flat or decline even after increases in the federal funds rate have begun. In the next subsection, we document this asymmetric sluggishness more formally by estimating some simple models.

B. Evidence of Sticky and Asymmetric Adjustment in Aggregate Data

We model the time-series behavior of aggregate deposit rates as depending on their own lagged values and on market interest rates. We estimate the regressions below over a sample that begins in July, 2000, the beginning of the most recent full easing cycle, and ends in July 2007, just before the recent financial turmoil began.

---

[9] The overall M2 rate, or "own rate," is calculated as the deposit-weighted average of rates paid on the major components of M2, which are liquid deposits, small time deposits, currency (zero), and retail money market mutual funds. The small time deposit rate is proxied by the six-month CD rate provided by Bankrate. "Liquid deposits" is the sum of checking and savings deposits, including MMDAs; this summation is done in order to control for the effects of sweeping, described in footnote 7 above. The liquid deposit rate is constructed based on Call Report and Bankrate data. Rates on money market mutual funds are provided by ICI.

Tables 1 and 2 present results for of the change in two aggregate Bankrate deposit rates, the MMDA rate and the six-month CD rate. These aggregate rates are constructed by Bankrate as the simple average of the rates offered by the top five banks in each of the top ten banking markets. The movements in these rates are regressed on their own lags and on the federal funds rate target and the three-month T-bill rate, with separate slope coefficients for periods when the federal funds rate target is rising or steady and for when it is falling. The three-month Treasury bill rate is commonly used in the computation of the opportunity cost of holding money, as it represents the rate on an asset that may be a close substitute to money and thus affects the demand for deposits. The target federal funds rate, which is highly correlated with the T-bill rate, is related to the marginal cost to the DI of an extra dollar of deposits, and thus influences the supply of deposits.[10][11] Both of these rates move essentially continuously and can be easily observed at a daily frequency.

In Table 1, the dependent variable is the change in the deposit rate (the commercial bank MMDA rate or six-month CD rate) and the independent variables are the lagged deposit rate, the change in the effective federal funds rate, and the change in the federal funds rate interacted with a dummy variable that is one when the change is positive or zero and zero otherwise.[12] A significant t-statistic on this last variable indicates that the response is asymmetric, or significantly different, when the rate is rising relative to the baseline of steady or falling rates.

---

[10] On deposits subject to reserve requirements, the federal funds rate is the cost to the DI of borrowing to fulfill the requirement (or the opportunity cost of holding reserves for DIs who do not need to borrow). Over this sample, the daily effective federal funds rate was, on average, within two basis points of the target and was seldom more than five basis points away from the target.

[11] One might consider the LIBOR or repo rate as well, but over the period in question, these rates are essentially identical to the effective federal funds rate.

[12] All t-statistics are computed using standard errors that are robust to heteroskedasticity and serial correlation in the errors.

The overall pace of deposit rate adjustment when market rates are rising can be calculated as the sum of the two coefficients on the market rates.

Table 1: Weekly Changes in Deposit Rates and FFR						
	BRM-CB MMDA Rate			BRM-6-Month CD Rate		
	Full	Early	Late	Full	Early	Late
Commercial bank MMDA rate, lag	-0.001+	-0.001	-0.004*			
	(-1.7)	(-0.1)	(-2.5)			
Fed funds target change	0.100*	0.111*	0.094*	0.384*	0.391*	0.371*
	-10	-2.5	-9.3	-18.9	-6.1	-16.2
Fed funds target rise	-0.055*	-0.043	-0.067*	-0.286*	-0.282*	-0.283*
	(-3.3)	(-0.9)	(-3.5)	(-8.3)	(-3.9)	(-6.5)
Commercial bank 6M CD rate, lag				-0.001	0.004	-0.004*
				(-1.1)	-0.9	(-3.4)
Constant	-0.001	-0.002	0.001	0.003	-0.016	0.009*
	(-0.6)	(-0.2)	-0.7	-1.1	(-0.7)	-2.6
Observations	551	181	370	551	181	370
R^2	0.18	0.08	0.24	0.41	0.23	0.45
Adjusted R^2	0.18	0.07	0.24	0.41	0.22	0.45

t statistics in parentheses
+ $p<0.10$, * $p<0.05$

For both deposit rate measurements, weekly adjustment to changes in the federal funds rate is far below unity, ranging from 10 basis points per percentage point of change for liquid deposit rates to 39 basis points per percentage point of change in the effective federal funds rate for small time deposits during times of stable or falling rates. Moreover, this stickiness is even stronger when the federal funds target is rising: for MMDA rates, the coefficient drops considerably, to 3 to 7 basis points per percentage point of change in the federal funds rate target; for the six-month CD rate, the coefficient drops to around 10 basis points per percentage point change in the federal funds rate target. Results are similar for the three-month bill rate, shown in

Table 2. Indeed, the regression results indicate that upward adjustments to savings rates are approximately zero at a weekly frequency when the federal funds target is rising.

Table 2: Weekly Changes in Deposit Rates and T-Bill rate						
	BRM-CB MMDA Rate			BRM-6-Month CD Rate		
	Full	Early	Late	Full	Early	Late
Commercial bank MMDA rate, lag	-0.002*	-0.003	-0.006*			
	(-2.1)	(-0.8)	(-3.6)			
3-month T-bill rate change	0.082*	0.011	0.083*	0.479*	0.205*	0.499*
	-5.9	-0.3	-5.6	-17.3	-3.1	-16.2
3-month T-bill rate change, FFR rising	-0.083*	-0.021	-0.083*	-0.390*	-0.177*	-0.363*
	(-4.8)	(-0.4)	(-4.2)	(-11.4)	(-2.5)	(-8.7)
Commercial bank 6M CD rate, lag				-0.001	0.009+	-0.004*
				(-0.6)	-1.7	(-3.1)
Constant	0.000	0.004	0.002	0.001	-0.039	0.007+
	(-0.2)	-0.5	-1.5	-0.4	(-1.6)	-2.0
Observations	551	181	370	551	181	370
R^2	0.07	0.01	0.13	0.37	0.07	0.47
Adjusted R^2	0.06	-0.01	0.13	0.37	0.06	0.46

t statistics in parentheses
+ $p<0.10$, * $p<0.05$

Much as slow adjustment of prices does not necessarily represent a cost to consumer because prices that are slow to rise can be advantageous to consumers, sticky deposit rates are not necessarily disadvantageous to consumers. Indeed, in the years of the financial crisis, a period beyond the sample examined in this period, deposit rates fell much more slowly than market rates, presumably benefiting depositors.[13] Nonetheless, when rates are slow to rise, the

---

[13] Indeed, the standard models of demand for M2 faced a considerable challenge in this period. The standard formulation of demand for M2 posits a relationship between the ratio of income to M2 and opportunity cost, or the difference between an alternative rate and the rate paid on M2. This rate is assumed to be positive, and yet it dropped well below zero as rates of adjustment on deposits lagged well behind the precipitous drops in market rates seen in late 2008 (see Judson, Schlusche, and Wong (2012 mimeo).

reductions in interest income to consumers can be considerable. Moreover, if the stickiness is asymmetric, as we show that it is for deposit rates, it is possible that the differences between actual and "equilibrium" or "nonsticky" rates could be costly to consumers on net.

Over the period examined here, we attempt a rough calculation as follows. First, following Moore, Porter, and Small (1989), we identify an equilibrium rate relationship by identifying periods of relatively stable deposit rates. These periods coincide (not surprisingly) with periods when the federal funds rate target had been stable for at least three months. We then estimate a least squares regression using these "equilibrium" observations and apply the coefficients to the whole sample. We then calculate the average difference between the actual and "equilibrium" rates. This rough calculation indicates that, over the sample period, actual deposit rates were about 15 to 25 basis points below actual rates. At current quantities of deposits, this difference would amount to an interest loss of about $15 billion (20 basis points x $7 trillion in savings in small time). These losses, however, are concentrated in times when rates are rising.

Looking forward, when interest rates lift off from their current levels near zero, these results suggest that deposit rates are likely to follow very slowly. Over the sample in this paper, the maximum gap between actual and "equilibrium" deposit rates was between 100 and 160 basis points; such a gap would represent a loss to consumers of about $70 billion to $100 billion per year. In the next section, we use the micro-level information to calculate the speed with which deposit rates are likely to rise when the target federal funds rate begins to lift off from its current near-zero level.

IV. Deposit Rate Behavior at Individual Branches

A. Durations between Rate Changes

1. Results

The results of the previous section show that at the aggregate level, deposit rates are sluggish and adjust symmetrically. In this section, we look at the adjustment of deposit rates at the depository institution (DI) branch level. Figure 3 plots histograms, by deposit type, of the average number of weeks between interest rate changes. For each DI branch, we compute the average by dividing the number of weeks the DI branch is in the sample by the number of interest rate changes observed. The first row displays histograms for 6-month and 24-month certificates of deposit (CDs) respectively.[14] The second row presents histograms for money market deposit accounts (MMDAs) and interest checking accounts, respectively. Insets in each chart give the medians of the average number of weeks between rate changes.

The charts in the first row show that CD rates change relatively quickly: the median number of weeks on average between rate changes ranges from 6.0 to 7.0, implying that rates change every month or two. The distribution across banks is fairly tight, and few banks average more than 15 weeks between changes for CD rates.

By contrast, the second rows shows considerably longer durations between interest rate changes for MMDAs (left panel) and interest-bearing checking accounts (right panel). The median average duration between price changes is about 20 weeks – or five months – for MMDAs and about 37 weeks—or about 9 months – for interest checking accounts. Moreover, there is much greater diversity in behavior across DI branches with these accounts than for CDs: over a quarter of DI branches change MMDA rates on average about every 8 months or less

---

[14] Maturities charted are 6 and 24 months. Data for 30-, 48-, and 84-month maturities are available in the dataset but are relatively sparse. Data for 3-, 12-, 36-, and 60-month maturities are similar and are available in an online appendix.

frequently, while about the same percentage of DI branches change interest checking rates on average yearly or less frequently.

2. Measuring the Degree of Deposit Rate Stickiness

As we noted above in our discussion of aggregate deposit rates, we would expect rates to move in response to changes in deposit demand and supply; thus, rates would be fully flexible if they changed at least as frequently as measured demand or supply shocks. Standard models of money demand suggest that deposit demand should depend on deposit opportunity cost, the difference between a short-term interest rate and the deposit rate. Since the 3-month T-bill rate, like other deposit rates, changes nearly continuously, fully flexible deposit rates should also adjust, at least to some extent, continuously.[15] Arguably, then, all deposit rates across all DI branches are sticky, since no DI branch on average changes any of its deposit rates at a weekly frequency.

It is possible that deposit demand itself responds sluggishly to changes in opportunity cost. Thus, the response of deposit rates to shocks to deposit supply may be a more accurate guide to how sticky deposit rates are. As noted above, the effective federal funds rate represents the marginal cost of an additional dollar of many kinds of transactions deposits. Moreover, bank prime lending rates, which in turn determine the pricing for many loans, are typically set as a fixed margin over the target federal funds rate. Hence the federal funds rate is an important determinant of both marginal cost and marginal revenue.

Over the 494 weeks of the sample period, the FOMC changed its target federal funds rate 39 times, implying an average time between changes of 12.6 weeks. By this standard, CD

---

[15] Deposit rates need not adjust by the full amount of the shock; doing so would complete undo the demand shock. However, if there is no adjustment in deposit rates—as appears to be the case here—then the adjustment is purely in quantities, suggesting a horizontal supply curve and thus completely sticky deposit rates.

rates are quite flexible, changing almost twice as frequently as the target federal funds rate; median MMDA rates change somewhat less often than the federal funds rate, though there is a long tail of DIs that change rates much less frequently; and interest checking rates are relatively sticky.

If we took as a criterion for having sticky deposit rates that a DI branch changed rates less frequently than the change in the target federal funds rate, then between about 5 to 20 percent of DI branches have sticky CD rates; about 75 percent have sticky MMDA rates; and over 90 have sticky interest checking rates.

Deposit rates are generally somewhat more flexible than goods prices; Klenow and Kryvstov (2008) and Nakamura and Steinsson (2006a) found that posted goods prices on average change about every four months; depending on how one accounts for sales, this figure can rise to eight months. However, deposit rates change much less frequently than the prices of many other financial assets that are alternative stores of value, such as equities or bonds (on the secondary market), which may change minute to minute.

3. Asymmetric Response of Deposit Rates to the Federal Funds Rate

From our results with the aggregate data, we suspect that there will likely be an asymmetric response of deposit rates to changes in the target federal funds rate, with faster responses to increases in the target than to decreases. We explore this hypothesis in Figure 4., where we break up the sample into time periods during which the federal funds rate is rising (left column), time periods during which it is falling (middle column), and periods during which it is flat (right column). The left and middle columns show histograms of the average number of weeks between rate changes during periods of falling and rising target federal funds rates respectively. It is immediately apparent that rates are much more flexible during periods of falling target rates. For CD rates, the median number of weeks between price changes ranges between 3 and 4 weeks during periods of falling target rates but around 74 weeks during periods of rising rates. In addition, the distributions are much more compressed during periods of falling rates. The same general pattern holds true for MMDAs and interest checking, though the distributions during periods of rising funds rate have much wider supports, with the average number of weeks between price changes exceeding two years for some DIs.

The right-hand column of Figure 4 shows the same data during periods where the target federal funds rate is flat. The rates generally show much greater median intervals between rate changes: for CDs, medians range between 7 and 9 weeks; for MMDAs, the median is 24 weeks, and for interest checking, 37 weeks. Moreover, the distributions in average rate changes across DI branches are wider, particularly in the cases of CD rates. Given the absence of a clearly important shock to deposit supply—federal funds rate changes—it is perhaps not surprising that durations between rate changes rise, although the high value of the median suggests that other shocks to deposit demand and supply may not be quantitatively important determinants of deposit rates. However, it is not clear to us why the dispersion in the distribution of average weeks between rate changes should rise.

4. Dynamic Response of Deposit Rates to Target Federal Funds Rate Changes

The results above show relatively sluggish responses of many deposit rates to changes in the target federal funds rate. In Figure 5, we further explore the dynamic path of responses to target rate increases and decreases. Each panel on the first page of figure 4 reports the cumulative fraction of DI branches to have made any change in its deposit rate following the 25 basis point increase in the target federal funds rate at the June 1999 FOMC meeting.[16] We plot the fractions for 26 weeks following the FOMC meeting; it is worth noting that another rate increase occurred at the next meeting, 7 weeks later. The charts show that only a very small fraction of DI branches make any change in their deposit rates in the week following the meeting—nearly zero in the case of interest checking and MMDAs, to about 20 percent for longer-maturity CD rates. For CD rates with maturities of more than 6 months, the fractions rise by nearly 10 percent per week, so that by the time of the next FOMC meeting, between 50 and 70 percent of DIs have adjusted their deposit rates. In contrast, MMDA and interest checking rates are extremely sluggish to change; by the time of the next FOMC meeting, only 10 to 20 percent of DIs have adjusted their rates.

The second page of Figure 8 shows comparable results for the January 2001 intermeeting decrease in the federal funds rate; in this case, the next decline occurred four weeks after the first decline.[17] A somewhat larger fraction of DI branches changed their CD rates immediately than in the case of the increase in the target rate. After four weeks, the vast majority of branches had changed their longer-maturity CD rates. Again in contrast, only a small fraction of branches changed their MMDA or interest checking rates in the weeks following the change.

Taken together, the results confirm that DI branches respond both sluggishly and asymmetrically to changes in the target federal funds rate. Moreover, the average fractions of price changes each week are quite low—even among the deposit rates for which branches are comparably more responsive to changes in the target federal funds rate, only about 10 percent per week of DI branches are changing rates.

---

[16] We choose that meeting because it was at the beginning of a tightening cycle; thus, deposit rates were not still responding to previous changes in the target federal funds rate.

[17] An additional feature of this change in the target rate was that it was likely more unexpected than other changes, since it did not occur during a regularly scheduled meeting.

5. Size of Deposit Rate Changes

We next look at the average size of rate increases and decreases. As in menu cost models, if infrequent deposit rate changes are caused by costs of changing rates, we should see relatively large rate changes. Figure 6 plots histograms of the size of rate increases (left-hand charts) and rate decreases (right-hand charts) by deposit types. As with prices of other goods, we see a fairly wide range of price changes, including some small changes. Median changes are in the 10 to 20 basis point range, comparable to the typical 25-basis-point sized change in the federal funds rate. The distributions of size by increases and decreases do not seem to differ in economically significant ways.

6. Differences by DI size

Finally, we look at the distribution of branch-level deposit rate changes by size of the parent DI, since larger institutions may act differently towards their customers than smaller ones. Figure 7 displays the same calculations as Figures 3 and 4, but for branches belonging to the top ten banks (by total deposits) in each time period.[18] A comparison of Figure 3 to Figure 7 shows that CD rates at large banks behave similarly to all banks: median durations between rate changes differ by a week or less. MMDA and interest checking rates appear to be somewhat more sluggish at larger banks. The median duration between rate changes for MMDA rates was 22.7 weeks at large banks and 20 weeks at all DIs; the figures for interest checking are 41.1 and 37.0 weeks, respectively. There also appears to be considerably more dispersion in the duration of interest rate changes at larger banks.

A comparison of Figures 4 and 7 shows that the difference in the number of weeks between rate changes across periods of rising and falling federal funds rates is greater for

---

[18] At the end of 2007, Call Report data showed that these institutions held about 30 percent of all interest checking deposits, half of all savings deposits, and 34 percent of all small time deposits.

branches of large DIs than for branches of all DIs. For example, the differences in median durations for MMDA rates across rising and falling periods are both about 13.7 and 23.7, compared with 12.7 and 20.8 weeks, respectively, for all DIs. On the whole, larger banks raise deposit rates more sluggishly during periods of rising federal funds rates.

Table 3: Median of average number of weeks between rate changes								
	Branches of top 10				Branches of top 10			
	Full sample	Fed funds rate falling	Fed funds target rising	Fed funds target flat	Full sample	Fed funds rate falling	Fed funds target rising	Fed funds target flat
6-month CD	7.0	3.8	6.8	9.8	7.1	3.5	6.7	8.6
24-month CD	6.0	3.4	7.4	7.3	5.5	2.9	8.0	6.0
MMDA	20.0	12.7	20.8	24.0	22.7	13.7	23.7	30.5
Interest checking	37.0	22.2	50.3	37.4	41.1	25.8	104.0	45.7

In contrast, a comparison of Figures 4 and 7 shows relatively little qualitative difference in average durations of rate changes between branches of larger DIs and branches of all DIs during periods where the federal funds rate is flat for CDs, though adjustment is more sluggish for MMDA and interest checking rates. A comparison of Figures 5 and 8 similarly shows relatively little difference in the distribution of the size of interest rate changes between large banks and all DIs.

Taken together with the above results for the rising and falling periods, it seems that larger DIs respond more strongly to changes in the federal funds rate than smaller DIs, but do not react in a different way to other deposit demand and supply shocks.

One other notable feature of these figures is that they contain far more than ten observations, since large DIs tend to have many branches. The still-considerable dispersion in the average duration of rate changes across DI branches thus indicates that deposit rate setting behavior varies across branches of the same institution. One might have thought *a priori* that there would be standard policies for each DI, and that we would therefore see clustering in the histograms around ten or fewer points.

Finally, these findings are broadly consistent with the aggregate regression results reported above: first, deposit rates are sticky, or adjust at a less than one-for-one pace to movements in market rates; second, the adjustment is asymmetric: coefficients of adjustment are significantly lower when the federal funds target and market rates are rising than when such rates are falling; third, rates are stickier for savings deposits than for time deposits.[19]

V. Relation to Previous Work on Deposit Rates

Several earlier papers have documented stickiness and asymmetric behavior in deposit rates. Hannan and Berger (1991) look at monthly observations on money market deposit accounts (MMDAs) of 398 banks from September 1983 to December 1986 from the Federal Reserve's Monthly Survey of Selected Deposits and Other Accounts. Hannan and Berger find that, of the 12,179 observations, 2,471 involved rate increases, 5,338 decreases, and 4,370 no rate change. They estimate multinomial logit models of the decision to change deposit rates, finding that banks have a 62 percent probability of reducing deposit rates in response to a decrease in the 3-month Treasury bill rate of 29 basis points (the mean absolute change over their sample), but only a 39 percent probability of raising rates in response to an equal-sized increase. They further show that banks in more concentrated markets have more rigid prices; larger banks have more flexible prices; and banks with larger market customer bases have less rigid prices.

---

[19] Results are similar when these regressions are estimated on aggregate M2, liquid deposit, and small time rates, which are deposit-weighted rather than simple averages and which cover virtually all deposits rather than only commercial bank MMDA and CD deposits.

Neumark and Sharpe (1992) look at the same survey, using monthly data on six-month certificates of deposits (CDs) and MMDAs for 255 banks from October 1983 through November 1987. They estimate a partial adjustment model, in which the long run deposit rates are assumed to be proportional to the six-month Treasury bill rate. The speed of adjustment is allowed to depend on concentration ratios and other market characteristics. They find that MMDA rates appear to adjust more sluggishly than CD rates. When rates are constrained to adjust symmetrically, concentration ratios appear to affect the long-run level of the markup of deposit rates over Treasury bill rates, but have little impact on the speed of adjustment. They estimate switching models to test for asymmetry in deposit rate setting. They find that rates adjust more slowly upwards than downwards, with banks in more concentrated markets being slower to adjust deposit rates upwards and faster to adjust deposit rates downwards. The long-run equilibrium markup is lower when asymmetry is allowed for.

Diebold and Sharpe (1990) examine the dynamic relationships among retail (deposit) rates and wholesale (federal funds and Treasury bill) rates. For deposit rates, they use weekly data on 6-month CDs, MMDAs, and super NOW (interest checking) accounts from Bank Rate Monitor (the predecessor of Bankrate, Inc.) from October 5, 1983 to December 25, 1985. The rates are averaged over 25 major banks and 25 major thrift institutions. They find that wholesale rates generally Granger-cause retail rates, but the latter do not Granger-cause the former. Retail rates have hump-shaped and persistent responses to innovations in wholesale rates. It takes about 2 weeks for one quarter of the response of retail rates to a shock to wholesale rates to manifest itself; about 5 weeks for half of the response, and about 10 weeks for three quarters of the response.

These four papers were written shortly after deposit rates were deregulated in the 1980s and were thus based on relatively short samples, making it difficult to precisely estimate the frequency of deposit rate adjustment. Moreover, during these earlier sample periods, changes in the target federal funds rate were not publicly announced, making it more difficult to evaluate the response of deposit rates to changes in this variable.

Craig and Dinger (2011) use Bankrate data, as we do, over about a ten-year period to document asymmetric stickiness in both deposit rates and in consumer loan rates. They estimate that the hazard rate of a change in deposit rate increases is hump-shaped with time, increasing for about the first six weeks before decreasing thereafter. They find that deposit-rate changes are also state-dependent, and that the hazards of changing deposit rates depend importantly on market share. Their paper uses a somewhat smaller sample than ours (624 branches as opposed to 2,500), and thus does not focus on differences in behavior across branches of the same institution. We also present results on the size of deposit-rate changes, on the aggregate behavior of deposit rates, and a simple model explaining aggregate stickiness.

Rosen (2002) develops a model with heterogeneous consumers (some of whom respond to lagged information) to explain asymmetries in deposit-rate stickiness (or indeed other kinds of price stickiness). He shows that the model is consistent with the behavior of deposit rates in a smaller set of data from Bankrate.

Yankov (2012) examines the behavior of CD rates over the most recent 15 years, 1997-2011, using data from RateWatch. He finds that dispersion of yields across institutions indicates monopoly power that is consistent with an asset-pricing model with varied search costs across consumers. Yankov's cross-section and time series are larger than in our paper, though his focus is on one particular type of deposit rate. His model takes an asset-pricing approach, in which demand for deposits is not related to the monetary services which they provide. His data source also does not have differences across bank branch.

VI. Modeling Asymmetric Deposit Rate Adjustment

The asymmetric sluggishness of deposit rates documented above is uncharacteristic of the behavior of prices of other kinds of financial assets. Equity prices vary tick-by-tick, and though yields on many, but not all, kinds of debt are constant until maturity, secondary-market yields and prices of debt also move continuously. However, prices of individual goods and services do show the same sort of asymmetric stickiness that deposit rates do. In this section, we first document other attempts to model deposit rates and goods prices. We then present a simple, static menu cost model of deposit rate setting, adapted from the literature on goods and service prices. We calibrate the model and show that, for reasonable parameter values, it can generate asymmetric, sluggish adjustment in deposit rates comparable to that seen in the data.[20]

A. A Simple Model of Asymmetric Deposit Rate Adjustment

In this section, we present a standard static menu-cost model of a bank that generates an asymmetric range of inaction in deposit rates around the optimum. There are N banks, indexed by i. Let D_t^i denote deposits held at bank i at time t, $r_t^{D,i}$ the interest rate paid on those deposits, and r_t^D the average deposit interest rate (so $r_t^D = \frac{1}{N}\sum r_t^{D,i}$) Suppose demand for deposits at bank i is given by:

$$D_t^i = \phi_D \left(1 + r_t^D - r_t^{D,i}\right)^{-\eta} (\phi_{OC}(1 + OC_t))^{-\psi}$$

where $OC_t = r_t^s - r_t^D$ is the opportunity cost of holding deposits, defined as the difference

---

[20] The model is monopolistically competitive, and thus also shows that the pattern of asymmetric stickiness does not require any collusive behavior among depository institutions.

between a short-term interest rate r_t^S and the average interest rate on deposits r_t^D, $\eta > 1$, and $\Psi > 1$. The first term in the demand function captures the degree to which bank i gains(loses) market share if its deposit rate is greater(less) than the average. The second term is a standard money demand function, in which demand for overall deposit holdings depends negatively on the opportunity cost of holding deposits relative to a short-term interest rate. Suppose that that rate is a constant markup μ^S over a market interest rate r_t^M such as the federal funds rate, so that $r_t^S = \mu^S + r_t^M$.

Suppose a bank's profit per unit of deposit—i.e. its net interest margin—is given by: $r_t^{L,i} - r_t^{D,i}$, where $r_t^{L,i}$ is the interest rate on loans (for simplicity, we ignore securities and other bank assets). Further suppose that loan rates are equal across banks and are a constant markup μ^L over the market rate, so that $r_t^L = \mu^L + r_t^M$. In practice, many loans are priced off of the prime rate, which is usually a 300 basis point markup over the target federal funds rate. Total bank profits are then given by:

$$\Pi_t = \left(\mu^L + r_t^M - r_t^{D,i}\right)\phi_D\left(1 + r_t^D - r_t^{D,i}\right)^{-\eta}(\phi_{OC}(1 + OC_t))^{-\psi}$$

Profit maximization (assuming the bank ignores its small effect on the average deposit rate) implies a deposit rate for bank i of:

$$r_t^{D,i} = \frac{1}{1-\eta}(1 + r_t^D) - \frac{\eta}{1-\eta}r_t^L$$

Which implies, in a symmetric equilibrium, that

$$r_t^{D,i} = r_t^D = r_t^L - \frac{1}{\eta}$$

Finally, suppose that the bank must pay a menu cost $z\Pi$ (i.e. one that is proportional to profits—a convenient normalization) if it wishes to adjust its deposit rate. In a static setting, it will only pay this cost if the change in profits in response to a shock exceeds the size of this menu cost.

Suppose $r^M_{t+1} = r^M_t + \delta$, where δ can be either positive or negative. To compute the range of inaction, we can compare the change in profits from adjusting, given no other bank adjusts, to not adjusting. This gain in profits $\Delta\Pi$ is:

$$\Delta\Pi = \left(\mu^L + r^M_{t+1} - r^{D,i}_{t+1}\right)\phi_D\left(1 + r^D_t - r^{D,i}_{t+1}\right)^{-\eta}(\phi_{OC}(1 + OC_{t+1}))^{-\psi}$$

$$- \left(\mu^L + r^M_{t+1} - r^{D,i}_t\right)\phi_D\left(1 + r^D_t - r^{D,i}_t\right)^{-\eta}(\phi_{OC}(1 + OC_{t+1}))^{-\psi}$$

Assuming we start at the symmetric equilibrium, this expression simplifies to:

$$\Delta\Pi = \left[\left(\frac{\delta}{1-\eta} + \frac{1}{\eta}\right)\left(1 + \frac{\eta\delta}{1-\eta}\right)^{-\eta} - \left(\delta + \frac{1}{\eta}\right)\right]\phi_D\left(\phi_{OC}(1 + \mu^S - \mu^L + \frac{1}{\eta} + \delta)\right)^{-\psi}$$

Bank i will adjust if the change in profits exceeds the menu cost.

Since $z\Pi = \left(\delta + \frac{1}{\eta}\right)\phi_D\left(\phi_{OC}(1 + \mu^S - \mu^L + \frac{1}{\eta} + \delta)\right)^{-\psi}$,

the condition for adjustment simplifies to:

$$\left(\frac{1}{\delta + \frac{1}{\eta}}\right)\left[\left(\frac{\delta}{1-\eta} + \frac{1}{\eta}\right)\left(1 + \frac{\eta\delta}{1-\eta}\right)^{-\eta}\right] \geq 1 + z$$

B. Calibration

We calibrate the model to determine whether there is an asymmetric range of inaction (with the downwards range being smaller than the upwards range) for a reasonable set of parameter values. We then see whether, for those values, we can match the sluggish rates of adjustment implied by both the aggregate and panel data. Given the model assumptions, the adjustment range depends only on the parameters η and z.

To pick the former, we note that the net interest margin is equal to $\frac{1}{\eta}$. We choose values between .01 and .05 to capture not just traditional net interest margins, but also broader concepts of profitability such as return on assets and narrower ones like returns on specific asset classes. We choose the menu cost z to be about one-half percent of profits, as in Nakamura and Steinsson. For all values of η, the adjustment range is smaller downwards than upwards by at least a few basis points, implying that the range of inaction is greater upwards than downwards, as predicted; the inaction ranges themselves range from -28 to +31 basis points for η=.01 and -48 to +51 basis points for η=.01. Moreover, these ranges exceed in absolute value the typical size for a federal funds rate change—25 basis points—suggesting that such a change would not induce all banks to change rates at once.

C. Other Models with Asymmetric, Sluggish Adjustment

Several researchers have attempted to develop models of asymmetric, sluggish price adjustment. Devereux and Siu (2007) calibrate a DSGE model with costs of changing prices which has the feature of asymmetric price adjustment. The gains to price adjustment are larger for positive than for negative shocks to marginal cost. In response to an increase in marginal costs, if all other firms raise their prices, but an individual firm does not, it receives more demand, but at a price now less than marginal cost, leading to large negative profits. For a negative shock, demand for a non-adjusting firm drops to zero; lowering its price will only increase its profits by a small amount. The degree of asymmetry depends on the effects of other firms' prices on demand for a firm's product and the extent to which prices are responsive to marginal cost. The authors are able to match their model to estimates they make of the asymmetric response of output to monetary policy.

Ellingsen, Friberg and Hassler (2006) derive conditions under which asymmetric price adjustment can be generated by menu cost models. Static models with constant elasticity of demand and a polynomial cost function with positive coefficients generate an asymmetric range of adjustment; these effects are third-order, and, though usually ruled out by the use of second-order approximations of the profit function, can be quantitatively important. The authors calibrate asymmetries large enough to be consistent with those in Peltzman (2000) in a dynamic model with inflation.

Tappata (2009) develops a search model with rational partially informed consumers to explain asymmetric price stickiness. In his model, consumers search more intensively when they expect the dispersion of prices to be higher—which in turn will occur when marginal cost is low rather than high. If shocks are persistent, when marginal cost is high, an unexpected drop in marginal cost will leave firms little incentive to lower prices, since consumers aren't searching very much. A rise in marginal cost when marginal cost is low will lead firms to be more responsive, since consumers will be searching intensively. In other words, the effect of other firms' prices on an individual firm's demand is greater for marginal cost increases than for decreases.

Much of this work has been inspired by empirical work documenting asymmetric and sluggish adjustment of other kinds of prices. Borenstein, Cameron and Gilbert (1997) show that retail gasoline prices respond more quickly to increases than to decreases in crude oil prices. They estimate that a 5 cent per gallon increase in crude oil prices costs a consumer $1.30 more over the life of the price adjustment than a 5 cent per gallon decrease saves her. They identify asymmetries in the costs of decreasing vs. increasing inventories and short-run market power of retailers as likely reasons for the asymmetry.

Peltzman (2000) documents asymmetries in the responses of output prices to input prices in micro data from the consumer and producer price indexes, for a total of 77 consumer and 165 producer goods. For both consumer and producer prices, after eight months a one percent increase in input costs leads to about a half percent increase in output price, but a one percent fall in input costs only reduces output prices by a bit more than one-third percent. Peltzman also establishes asymmetric responses in the prices of a supermarket chain, which are more pronounced for goods with a diverse set of wholesalers or volatile input prices.

D. Other Work on Price Adjustment

Our work is also related to papers that document price stickiness at the microeconomic level. That work has found a high degree of diversity in the duration of price changes across goods. Cecchetti (1985) found that magazine prices change every 1½ to 3¼ years. Lach and Tsiddon (1991) showed that food prices in Israeli supermarkets change every 1.9 months to 1.6 months during periods of high inflation. Kashyap (1995) reported that the average time between price changes on retail goods in catalogs 15 months, with longer intervals not unusual. Carlton (1986) show that data from Stigler and Kindahl (1970) on individual transactions prices for industrial goods indicate average durations of price stickiness of 6.5 months, with, again, many prices changing even less frequently.. Levy and Young (2004) document that the price of a 6.5 ounce bottle of Coca Cola remained at 5 cents for more than 70 years (1886-1959).

Several more recent studies have used the data underlying the computation of the consumer price index to show price stickiness for a broader range of goods. Bils and Klenow (2004) calculate an average duration of price changes of 4.3 months, or 5.5 months including sales. The duration of price stickiness again differs substantially across price categories. Nakamura and Steinsson (2006a) find slightly different results. They document that: the median duration of price changes to be 11 months, or 8.7 months for finished goods prices[21]; one third of price changes are price decreases.; the frequency of price increases responds to inflation, while frequency of price decreases and size of price increases and decreases does not; price changes are highly seasonal (largest in the first quarter, smallest in the fourth quarter); and the hazard function for price changes is downward sloping for first few months, and flat thereafter, except for a large spike at 12 months in consumer services. Nakamura and Steinsson (2006b) use the results of this paper to evaluate the ability of different kinds of price adjustment models to fit the data. Klenow and Kryvtsov (2005) find a wide distribution of price changes, with some prices changing monthly while others taking more than 5 years to change.

In our current paper, we find that deposit rates change relatively more frequently than prices, with median durations of price changes across DIs of about 1 month for CD rates, 3 months for MMDAs, and nearly 5 months for interest checking accounts. The frequency of rate increases or decreases is linked to the frequency of target federal funds rate changes; since rates decrease more rapidly than they increase, in long-run equilibrium it is likely that interest rate increases will be more frequent than decreases.

E. Goods and Service Prices vs. Asset Prices

A simple model of goods and service prices accounts for some key features of deposit rate behavior. This raises the question of why deposits are more like goods and services in this respect than they are like other financial assets. One possibility is that, unlike other financial assets, deposits provide monetary services (also known as liquidity or transactions services). The asymmetric sluggishness of rates may be an outcome of the factors which move the market

---

[21] Part of the difference between their results and those of Bils and Klenow arises from the definition of a sale or a temporary price change.

for monetary services. The extensive literature on money demand has inversely linked the opportunity cost of holding deposits—the difference between the rate on some non-monetary financial asset and the deposit rate—to the level of monetary services provided.[22] To the extent that deposits' provisions of monetary services is leading to their asymmetric stickiness, one would expect such stickiness to be greater for assets which provide more monetary services—i.e. those with greater opportunity costs, or lower rates. Our findings are consistent with that prediction—deposit rates on MMDAs and interest checking accounts are both lower and stickier than rates on CDs.

VII. Conclusion

We use a panel dataset of over 2,500 branches of about 900 depository institutions (DIs) observed weekly over ten years to examine the dynamics of changes in interest rates on interest checking accounts, MMDAs, and nine different maturities of CDs. We have six key findings. First, some deposit rates are more flexible than others. CD rates are quite flexible, with the median branch changing such rates every 6 weeks on average, while MMDA and interest checking rates show much more inertia, changing every 20 weeks and 37 weeks on average, respectively. Second, the frequency of rate changes exhibits considerable dispersion for some types of deposits, with about a quarter of institutions changing interest checking rates twice a year or less frequently. Third, deposit rate changes are asymmetric: rates adjust about twice as frequently during periods of falling target federal funds rate than rising ones. Fourth, rates are uniformly quite sticky during periods when the federal funds rate is flat, with median durations between price changes ranging from 8 weeks to 39 weeks. Fifth, the median size of rate changes

---

[22] See Barnett, Fisher, and Serletis (1992) for a survey on the microeconomics of demand for monetary services, and Rotemberg, Driscoll, and Poterba (1995) for one example.

is about 11 to 23 basis points, comparable to the typical 25 basis point change in the target federal funds rate; the distribution of average decreases and increases is about the same, and is relatively dispersed, with many small changes of a few basis points. Sixth, there is greater upward stickiness in rates on interest checking and money market accounts for branches of large DIs than for smaller ones.

These results taken together confirm and extend the earlier findings of Hannan and Berger (1990), Diebold and Sharpe (1990), and Neumark and Sharpe (1992) on smaller and shorter datasets, and complement those of Craig and Dinger (2011) and Yankov (2012).

We have two additional results. First, we show that a simple menu cost model is consistent with the asymmetric stickiness observed here. Second, we show that, even in the aggregate, deposit rates are sticky, and we estimate some simple models of aggregate rate adjustment. We use these estimates to show that, when the federal funds rate lifts off from its current level near zero, deposit rates are likely to follow very slowly, and that depositors could earn as much as $100 billion less per year relative to what would occur if deposit rates were not asymmetrically sticky. Of course, these extra payments would come at the expense of bank revenues, and stickiness of deposit quantities may enhance financial stability. In addition, low policy rates, by boosting aggregate demand, may have other beneficial effects, so the net welfare effects of a low interest rate environment are not solely determined by the effects on deposit holders.

REFERENCES

Barnett, William A., Douglas Fisher, and Apostolos Serletis (1992). "Consumer Theory and the Demand for Money." *Journal of Economic Literature*, 30(4), pp. 2086-2119.

Barro, Robert J. (1972). "A Theory of Monopolistic Price Adjustment." *Review of Economic Studies*, 39(1), pp. 17-26.

Bils, Mark and Peter J. Klenow (2004). "Some Evidence on the Importance of Sticky Prices." *Journal of Political Economy*, 112(5), pp. 947-985.

Bricker, Jesse, Arthur B. Kennickell, Kevin B. Moore and John Sabelhaus (2012). "Changes in U.S. Family Finances from 2007 to 2010: Evidence from the Survey of Consumer Finances." *Federal Reserve Bulletin*, 98(2), pp. 1-80.

Calvo, Guillermo (1983). "Staggered Prices in a Utility-Maximizing Framework." *Journal of Monetary Economics*, 12(5), pp. 1659-1686.

Carlton, Dennis W. (1986). "The Rigidity of Prices." *The American Economic Review*, 76 (September), pp. 637-658.

Cecchetti, Stephen G. (1985). "Staggered Contracts and the Frequency of Price Adjustment." *Quarterly Journal of Economics*, 100(Supplement), pp. 935-959.

Craig, Ben R., and Valeriya Dinger (2011). "The Duration of Bank Retail Interest Rates." Federal Reserve Bank of Cleveland Working Paper 10-01R.

Diebold, Francis X. and Steven A. Sharpe (1990). "Post-Deregulation Bank-Deposit-Rate Pricing: The Multivariate Dynamics." *Journal of Business & Economic Statistics*, 8(3), pp. 281-291.

Dotsey, Michael, Robert G. King and Alexander Wolman (1999). "State-Dependent Pricing and the General Equilibrium Dynamics of Money and Output." *Quarterly Journal of Economics*, 114(3), pp. 655-690.

Eichenbaum, Martin, Nir Jaimovich and Sergio Rebelo (2008). "Reference Prices and Nominal Rigidities." Working paper, Northwestern University.

Gertler, Mark and John Leahy (2009). "A Phillips Curve with an *Ss* Foundation." *Journal of Political Economy*, 116(3), pp. 533-572.

Golosov, Mikhail and Robert E. Lucas Jr., (2007). "Menu Costs and Phillips Curves." *Journal of Political Economy*, 1152), pp. 171-199.

Hannan, Timothy H. and Allen N. Berger (1991). "The Rigidity of Prices: Evidence from the Banking Industry." *The American Economic Review*, 81(4), pp. 938-945.

Kashyap, Anil K. (1995). "Sticky Prices: New Evidence from Retail Catalogs." *Quarterly Journal of Economics* 110(2), pp. 245-274.

Kiley, Michael T. (2000). "Endogenous Price Stickiness and Business Cycle Persistence." *Journal of Money, Credit, and Banking*, 32(1), pp. 28-53.

Klenow, Peter and Oleksiy Kryvstov (2008). "State-Dependent or Time-Dependent Pricing: Does It Matter for Recent U.S. Inflation?" Working paper, Stanford University.

Lach, Saul and Dani Tsiddon (1992). "The Behavior of Prices and Inflation: An Empirical Analysis of Disaggregated Price Data." *Journal of Political Economy*, 100(2), pp. 349-389.

Levy, Daniel and Andrew T. Young (2004) "'The Real Thing': Nominal Price Rigidity of the Nickel Coke, 1886-1959." *Journal of Money, Credit and Banking*, 36(4), pp. 765-799.

Lucas, Robert E. Jr. (1972), "Expectations and the Neutrality of Money." *Journal of Economic Theory*, 4(1), pp. 103-124.

Mankiw, N. Gregory (1985). "Small Menu Costs and Large Business Cycles: A Macroeconomic Model of Monopoly." *Quarterly Journal of Economics*, 100(3), pp. 529-539.

----- and Ricardo Reis (2002). "Sticky Information Versus Sticky Prices: A Proposal to Replace the New Keynesian Phillips Curve." *Quarterly Journal of Economics*, 117(6), pp. 1295-1328.

Nakamura, Emi and Jon Steinsson (2006a). "Five Facts About Prices: A Reevaluation of Menu Cost Models." Working paper, Columbia University.

-----(2006b). "Monetary Non-Neutrality in a Multi-Sector Menu Cost Model." Working paper, Columbia University.

Neumark, David and Steven A. Sharpe (1992). "Market Structure and the Nature of Price Rigidity: Evidence from the Market for Consumer Deposits." *Quarterly Journal of Economics*, 107(2), pp. 657-680.

Rice, Tara N. and Evren Ors (2006). "Bank Imputed Interest Rates: Unbiased Estimates of Offered Rates?" Working Paper, Federal Reserve Bank of Chicago.

Rotemberg, Julio (1982). "Monopolistic Price Adjustment and Aggregate Output." *Review of Economic Studies*, 58(4), pp. 517-531.

-----, John C. Driscoll and James M. Poterba (1995). "Money, Output, and Prices: Evidence from a New Monetary Aggregate." *Journal of Business & Economic Statistics,* 13(1), pp. 67-83.

Stigler, George and James Kindahl (1970). *The Behavior of Individual Prices.* National Bureau of Economic Research, General Series, no. 90. New York: Columbia University Press.

Taylor, John B. (1980). "Aggregate Dynamics and Staggered Contracts." *Journal of Political Economy*, 88(1), pp. 1-24.

Yankov, Vladimir (2012). "In Search of a Risk-Free Asset." Working Paper, Federal Reserve Bank of Boston.

www.ingramcontent.com/pod-product-compliance
Lightning Source LLC
Chambersburg PA
CBHW081810170526
45167CB00008B/3393